More Mirrors

More Mirrors

Affirmations & Actions for Daily Reflection

Cheryl Wall

YES INTERNATIONAL PUBLISHERS
St. Paul, Minnesota

Also by Cheryl Wall:
Mirrors: Affirmations & Actions for Daily Reflection

Printed in the United States of America

ISBN: 0-936663-05-7
Library of Congress Catalog Number 91-65477

YES International Publishers
P.O. Box 75032, St. Paul, MN 55175

More Mirrors
Affirmations and Actions for Daily Reflection

More Mirrors means more fun, more self discovery, and more insights as you travel your own path of spiritual growth. Each affirmation or activity is designed to help you grow in self esteem and connect to Spirit. Even though these activities will only take a few minutes of your day, you'll find they have a profound influence on your life.

How often have you looked into your mirror and asked, "Who am I?" In this workbook, you'll find plenty of positive ways to see yourself.

If you've used the first *Mirrors* workbook, you already know the power of seeing esteem-building affirmations at the same time you see your own image in the mirror. It is as though you've tattooed something positive on your forehead to carry with you always. To write the affirmations on the mirror, use a water based pen such as ones used to write on overhead transparencies or whiteboards.

In *More Mirrors,* you'll find insights and fun, thought provoking quotations, and new ways to view your life. Some weeks you'll focus on one theme, such as forgiveness or your power of choice. Other weeks, you'll spread your focus to a variety of themes. *More Mirrors* will help you establish a pattern of behavior and thought that defines your personal spirituality.

This workbook is an excellent support for any therapeutic programs, such as twelve step programs or individual therapy of all types. It is also an excellent workbook for *any* individual who wants to establish positive self esteem and spirituality as part of her or his daily life.

Enjoy the weeks and months to come. I wish you peace, joy, love, and healing as we all progress on our paths in life.

Cheryl Hall

Dates:

Monday

Write this on your mirror: I am happy.

Tuesday

Read the peace invocation on the opposite page. What does it mean to you today?

Wednesday

Write this on your mirror: I choose to see goodness surrounding me.

Thursday

Call a friend and share one reason why the friendship you share is so valuable.

Friday

Write this on your mirror: I am trustworthy.

Saturday

Take a walk today and focus your attention on how others have contributed to your style of living.

Sunday

Write this on your mirror: I am inspired by the beauty of all creation.

Peace Invocation

From the Power of Love
within the glory of God
let Love stream forth
into the hearts of all.

From the Power of Peace
within the center of God
let Peace flow forth
into the minds of all.

Let Father Spirit and Mother Earth
restore Love and Peace on our good earth.

My love is God's Love and our Love
is bringing peace on earth.

With Love and Peace,
go my friend, and
share this message
to the end.

Prince Hirindra Singh, Ph.D.

Dates:

Monday

Make an effort to eat slowly today, relishing the flavors and textures of your food.

Tuesday

Write this on your mirror: I have high aspirations.

Wednesday

On the opposite page, list three goals you have for your inner self.

Thursday

Write this on your mirror: I am fun to be with.

Friday

Send a silly card to a friend or loved one.

Saturday

Write this on your mirror: I encourage myself to live fully.

Sunday

This evening, find a place to gaze at the stars. Think about how vast, beautiful, and amazing our galaxy is.

Dates:

Monday

Write this on your mirror: I am radiant.

Tuesday

As you shower or bathe today, take time to enjoy how the water feels against your back, your hands, your chest, your legs, and your face.

Wednesday

Write this on your mirror: I am witty.

Thursday

On the opposite page, list four ways you've brought smiles to people's faces.

Friday

Write this on your mirror: I take care of myself because I love myself.

Saturday

Buy or borrow a book a friend has recommended. Begin reading it today.

Sunday

Write this on your mirror: I choose to nourish my soul with love, beauty, and kindness.

Dates:

Monday

What one spiritual practice from your youth was meaningful to you? Practice it today or the first appropriate day this week.

Tuesday

Write this on your mirror: I am courageous.

Wednesday

On the opposite page, describe a time when your courage helped you through a crisis.

Thursday

Write this on your mirror: I see many options and make good choices.

Friday

What does "freedom" mean to you? During this day, focus on the freedoms you have and how you choose to exercise them.

Saturday

Write this on your mirror: I am gracious.

Sunday

When people pay you compliments, accept them with thanks and do not deny their good opinion.

Dates:

Monday

Write this on your mirror: I am gentle.

Tuesday

Find a place where you can be uninterrupted for ten minutes. Sit quietly and breathe gently and deeply. On each exhalation, repeat softly, "Forgiveness is mine."

Wednesday

Write this on your mirror: I am self confident.

Thursday

This morning, think of the choices you'll make today. Remind yourself that each choice -- large or small -- is yours and only yours to make.

Friday

Write this on your mirror: I am powerful over my own life.

Saturday

Follow the directions on the opposite page to deal with a situation from the past that troubles you.

Sunday

Write this on your mirror: I am tranquil.

Forgiveness for the Past

In the space below, write about a situation from the past that still troubles you.

In the first paragraph, describe the situation.

In the second paragraph, write how and why you acted or reacted as you did. Remember that you didn't know then what you do know now. Focus on what was happening and what you knew then.

In the third paragraph, write forgiveness for yourself and the others involved.

Dates:

Monday

When you go shopping this week, think carefully about how your purchases affect the environment. Let your choices reflect concern for the earth.

Tuesday

Write this on your mirror: I am cheerful.

Wednesday

Each time you drink water today, repeat to yourself, "I cleanse myself of wastes and toxins."

Thursday

Write this on your mirror: I deserve and appreciate my warm, loving friends.

Friday

What would you really like a loved one to do for you? Make plans now to do it for yourself.

Saturday

Write this on your mirror: I learn new things all the time.

Sunday

Read the quote by Joan Didion on the opposite page. What does it mean for you today?

Character -- the willingness
to accept responsibility for
one's own life -- is the source
from which self-respect springs.

Joan Didion

Dates:

Monday

Write this on your mirror: I sparkle with good health.

Tuesday

Place your hand over your heart. Slowly move your hand counter clockwise. Continue this massage for five minutes and imagine healing warmth flowing from your hand to your body.

Wednesday

Write this on your mirror: I have a wonderful imagination.

Thursday

On the opposite page, write what your "guardian angel" would be like. Describe what she or he could look like, what she or he might say to you, and how she or he helps you.

Friday

Write this on your mirror: I am attractive and charming.

Saturday

Sit quietly. Very gently, use your fingertips to slowly explore your face. Use a full ten minutes to learn each curve and plane.

Sunday

Write this on your mirror: I recognize welcome good luck into my life.

Dates:

Monday

On the opposite page, list one thing you wish to be free from. Then list three things you can do to bring about that freedom.

Tuesday

Write this on your mirror: I am made in the image of God's perfection.

Wednesday

Light a candle and dedicate its light to something you believe is important. Allow the candle to completely burn away.

Thursday

Write this on your mirror: I am filled with joy.

Friday

Tonight, howl at the moon like a wolf. Consider the idea that howling might be a way wolves celebrate nature's glory.

Saturday

Write this on your mirror: I help others see good in the world.

Sunday

Write a complimentary letter to a store or person who provided good customer service to you recently. Be as specific as possible.

Dates:

Monday

Write this on your mirror: I am like a blooming, beautiful flower.

Tuesday

Buy or gather flowers for your work area. Make a point to smell them several times a day.

Wednesday

Write this on your mirror: I am brave.

Thursday

Write a note about a trait you admire about yourself. Post it on your refrigerator.

Friday

Write this on your mirror: I am intelligent.

Saturday

On the opposite page, write five ways you've made smart decisions this week.

Sunday

Write this on your mirror: I choose the best course of action for my circumstances.

Dates:

Monday

If you have a telephone answering machine, call it and leave a message about how wonderful you are. If you don't have a machine, write yourself a note.

Tuesday

Write this on your mirror: I am a sympathetic listener.

Wednesday

Encourage a friend or loved one to forgive herself or himself for something she or he has regretted for a long time.

Thursday

Write this on your mirror: I am glad to be me.

Friday

Take a walk today. Focus your attention on the shapes of trees and shrubs.

Saturday

Write this on your mirror: I like to try new things.

Sunday

Read the quote from the Tao Te Ching on the opposite page. What does it mean to your life?

Heaven is long enduring and earth continues long. The reason why heaven and earth are able to endure and continue thus long is because they do not live of, or for, themselves. This is how they are able to continue and endure.

Lao Tzu
Tao Te Ching

Dates:

Monday

Write this on your mirror: I am dazzling when I smile.

Tuesday

As you eat vegetables in today's meals, consider that you are eating stored sunlight.

Wednesday

Write this on your mirror: I enjoy learning about myself.

Thursday

On the opposite page, write a paragraph or two about a time you recognized that you and another loved each other (either romantically, familialy, or as a friend). Include details.

Friday

Write this on your mirror: I have good judgment.

Saturday

Sit quietly for ten minutes, breathing slowly and deeply through both your nose and mouth. Focus all your thoughts on the feeling of your breath against your nostrils and lips.

Sunday

Write this on your mirror: My spirit grows stronger every day.

Dates:

Monday

Write yourself a glowing review of your latest project (big or small). Mail it to yourself at the place where you did the work.

Tuesday

Write this on your mirror: I am enthusiastic.

Wednesday

Deliver an inexpensive, but fun gift to a friend who least expects it.

Thursday

Write this on your mirror: I am quick witted.

Friday

What would the world be like if you had never been in it? Take fifteen minutes to think of the richness you've added to the lives of friends, family, and acquaintances.

Saturday

Write this on your mirror: My eyes beam love for the world.

Sunday

On the opposite page, create a prayer for one or more people you know who are in need of Divine assistance.

Dates:

Monday

Write this on your mirror: I am contented.

Tuesday

Take ten minutes to close your eyes and breathe slowly and deeply. At each exhalation, repeat, "I am free."

Wednesday

Write this on your mirror: My body works with efficiency and strength.

Thursday

Put slow music on the radio or stereo. Dance with slow, stretching movements and try to feel the perfection of your muscles.

Friday

Write this on your mirror: I hold myself in high regard.

Saturday

On the opposite page, draw the outline of your hand. Now carefully add the details that make your hand unique.

Sunday

Write this on your mirror: I am a force for good in the world.

Dates:

Monday

This week when problems arise, resist urges you may have to blame or find fault. Instead, focus on the problem's resolution.

Tuesday

Write this on your mirror: I have a fascinating personality.

Wednesday

On the opposite page, describe your unique style.

Thursday

Write this on your mirror: My choices show that I care about my life.

Friday

Today, choose foods and beverages that you know are both nourishing and free from toxins.

Saturday

Write this on your mirror: I am adorable.

Sunday

Make faces at yourself in the mirror. Smile, grin, flirt, and play with your image.

Dates:

Monday

Write this on your mirror: I am thoughtful.

Tuesday

Take ten minutes to sit quietly. Visualize the planet earth with beautiful white light surrounding it and bathing it in Divine Love.

Wednesday

Write this on your mirror: There is unlimited potential for happiness in my life.

Thursday

Read the words of Hannah Arendt on the opposite page. How do they apply to your life?

Friday

Write this on your mirror: I am clever.

Saturday

Find your favorite place in your home. Examine how you've decorated and arranged things. Admire the ambiance of what you've created.

Sunday

Write this on your mirror: I am artistic.

Forgiveness is the key
to action and freedom.

Hannah Arendt

Dates:

Monday

On the opposite page, write one reason you are a good friend.

Tuesday

One the opposite page, write one reason your work is so important.

Wednesday

On the opposite page, write one reason a family member loves you.

Thursday

On the opposite page, write one reason you are glad to be yourself.

Friday

On the opposite page, write one reason your community is lucky to have you.

Saturday

On the opposite page, write one way those close to you can rely on you.

Sunday

Read all the statements you've written on the opposite page. Now take five minutes to reflect on what you add to others' lives.

Dates:

Monday

Write this on your mirror: My mind is free to think without prejudice.

Tuesday

What are you curious about? Go to a library or bookstore and get a book about the subject.

Wednesday

Write this on your mirror: I am adventurous.

Thursday

Follow the directions on the opposite page to address a habit you'd like to change.

Friday

Write this on your mirror: I am willing to try new things.

Saturday

Sit quietly and comfortably. Imagine a cleansing, white flame slowly climbing from the base of your spine through the top of your head.

Sunday

Write this on your mirror: Everything I learn adds to my ability to feel joy.

Goodbye to a Habit

We would not develop a habit unless at one time it had served us or given us something. In order to stop the habit, we need to honor what it once did. Use the space below to explore the origins of your habit and to release yourself from its grasp.

First, describe the habit. Second, describe how it started. Third, thank it for what it provided you in the beginning. Fourth, explain why it is no longer useful to you. Finally, say goodbye to it and describe its disappearance.

Dates:

Monday

Write a letter or post card to one of your political representatives. Give him or her your views on a current topic.

Tuesday

Write this on your mirror: I am honorable.

Wednesday

Read the passage from Psalms on the opposite page. What does this mean within your household?

Thursday

Write this on your mirror: I can explore many points of view without fear.

Friday

Think about someone who has a completely different viewpoint from your own. Take ten minutes to explore how they may have come to hold that viewpoint.

Saturday

Write this on your mirror: I love myself unconditionally.

Sunday

Ask a friend or loved one to trade neck rubs. Take a moment to think about how people can help each other feel good.

I will walk with integrity
of heart within my house;
I will not set before my eyes
anything that is base.

Psalms 101:3

Dates:

Monday	Write this on your mirror: I have feelings, and I am more than my feelings.
Tuesday	What makes you feel emotional? Promise yourself that the next time you experience such emotions, you will allow them to flow freely.
Wednesday	Write this on your mirror: I have a body, and I am more than my body.
Thursday	Allow yourself twice as long as usual to eat your meals. Use this extra time to allow even more enjoyment of the earth's bounty.
Friday	Write this on your mirror: I have intelligence, and I am more than my intelligence.
Saturday	On the opposite page, write about two ways your intelligence served you well this week.
Sunday	Write this on your mirror: My spirit is strong, and I have access to an infinite source of spiritual strength.

Dates:

Monday

Read "Margaret's Rules" on the opposite page. How can you follow these rules?

Tuesday

Write this on your mirror: My talents bring joy to others.

Wednesday

Send a humorous card to someone who could use a good laugh.

Thursday

Write this on your mirror: I am a catalyst for joy among my friends.

Friday

Call a friend or loved one and make plans to do something while enjoying nature.

Saturday

Write this on your mirror: I accept the gifts of joy that others give to me.

Sunday

Allow someone to help you with a task you normally do yourself.

Margaret's Rules

1. First and foremost, I take care of myself.

2. I leave laughter and joy behind me.

3. I do nice things for people when I can.

Margaret Bedor

Dates:

Monday

Write this on your mirror: I make shrewd decisions.

Tuesday

On the opposite page, list six things you like to do and that you do well.

Wednesday

Write this on your mirror: I can relax without guilt.

Thursday

Light a stick or cone of incense. As it burns, allow yourself to think about nothing but the shapes of the smoke and the smell of the scent.

Friday

Write this on your mirror: I deserve joy in my life.

Saturday

Clean out a closet, junk drawer, or cluttered shelf. Get rid of everything that is no longer of use or value to you.

Sunday

Write this on your mirror: There is an abundance of pleasure for me to receive.

Dates:

Monday

Think about a friendship or relationship from your past that ended badly. Close your eyes and say three times out loud, "(Person's Name), I forgive you."

Tuesday

Write this on your mirror: I choose friends who support my personal growth.

Wednesday

Call two or three people you enjoy and make plans to make dinner together.

Thursday

Write this on your mirror: I deserve happiness.

Friday

On the opposite page, write your thoughts about a choice you've made that altered your life for the better.

Saturday

Write this on your mirror: I am amazing.

Sunday

Take a walk or run today at a slightly higher pace than usual. Congratulate yourself for stretching your physical limits.

Dates:

Monday

Write this on your mirror: I project radiance to all.

Tuesday

Read the Buddhist Meditational Prayer on the opposite page out loud.

Wednesday

Write this on your mirror: My body shines with health.

Thursday

Sit quietly for ten minutes. Place your fingertips on a pulse point and free your mind from all thoughts but the beat of your heart.

Friday

Write this on your mirror: My thoughts brighten conversations.

Saturday

When you are outside today, pause a moment or more to let the sun shine on you. During that time, try to think of nothing but the feeling of sunlight shining on you.

Sunday

Write this on your mirror: I am a force for enlightenment.

The Four Immeasurable Thoughts

May all sentient beings have happiness and the cause of happiness;

May all sentient beings be free from suffering and the causes of suffering;

May all sentient beings never be separated from the happiness that knows no suffering;

May all sentient beings abide in equanimity, free from attachment and anger, which hold some close and others distant.

Buddhist Meditational Prayer

Dates:

Monday

Wear your favorite cologne or perfume every day this week.

Tuesday

Write this on your mirror: I deserve prosperity.

Wednesday

What do you think "abundance of the universe" means? Think about it today. This afternoon or evening discuss it with someone whose opinion you value.

Thursday

Write this on your mirror: The work I do assists many people's lives.

Friday

Make a gift of time or money to an organization which supports the natural environment.

Saturday

Write this on your mirror: I am proud of my contributions to my community.

Sunday

On the opposite page, list three ways you've helped others recently.

Dates:

Monday

Write this on your mirror: I can accept compliments easily because they are true.

Tuesday

On the opposite page, write your wish for your future.

Wednesday

Write this on your mirror: I am filled with positive energy.

Thursday

Take ten minutes to sit quietly. Imagine yourself in a garden. Notice as many details as you can. What do the things in your garden symbolize about your life?

Friday

Write this on your mirror: My priorities are good and appropriate for my life.

Saturday

What is your favorite food? Create a short, fun ritual to honor it as you prepare it and eat it.

Sunday

Write this on your mirror: I have integrity.

Dates:

Monday

Write a problem you are troubled by on a piece of paper. Crumple the paper, place it in a fireproof container and burn it. As it burns, express your intention to turn the problem over to God.

Tuesday

Write this on your mirror: My sad feelings can also serve to teach me important lessons.

Wednesday

Read the words of M.K. Gandhi on the opposite page. What do they mean to you today?

Thursday

Write this on your mirror: I am a part of all creation.

Friday

Find ten minutes to breathe calmly and deeply. When you feel very relaxed, imagine a beam of energy flowing from the earth, through your body, and up toward the stars.

Saturday

Write this on your mirror: I free myself from a limited viewpoint.

Sunday

As you shower or bathe today, imagine that the water is cleansing your spirit as well as your body.

Freedom is not worth having if it
it does not connote freedom to err.

M.K. Gandhi

Dates:

Monday

Write this on your mirror: I appreciate all the signs of God's magnificence.

Tuesday

On the opposite page, list five things you are awestruck by in the natural world.

Wednesday

Write this on your mirror: I have a great sense of humor.

Thursday

Put yourself in a situation you know will make you laugh. Feel your laughter dissolve tensions in your face and body.

Friday

Write this on your mirror: I notice the little things that make life joyful.

Saturday

Tonight before you sleep, visualize a perfect day. Think of at least seven things that make it perfect.

Sunday

Write this on your mirror: I attract fun.

Dates:

Monday

Send warm thoughts of love and encouragement to someone who has a tough decision to make.

Tuesday

Write this on your mirror: I support others' growth and development.

Wednesday

On the opposite page, write what you think it means to "love someone without expectations."

Thursday

Write this on your mirror: I like to make people feel good about themselves.

Friday

Make plans with a friend or loved one who shares your sense of humor to go to (or rent) a funny move, see a funny play, or attend a comedy show.

Saturday

Write this on your mirror: I am a source for renewal.

Sunday

Watch a television program or a movie that teaches you something about the natural world.

Dates:

Monday

Write this on your mirror: I deserve to be treated well.

Tuesday

What would you consider one act of good self indulgence? Make plans to do it for yourself.

Wednesday

Write this on your mirror: I find peace within myself.

Thursday

Read the Forgiveness Prayer on the opposite page out loud.

Friday

Write this on your mirror: I choose to have an open mind.

Saturday

Make plans with a friend or loved one to share a meal with foods or cooking styles that are new to you.

Sunday

Write this on your mirror: Freedom is the Creator's gift to me.

Forgiveness Prayer

I forgive myself.

I am a growing, learning being. I know more today than I knew before. Tomorrow I will know even more.

I forgive that I did not know it all before; I forgive that I do not know it all right now.

I am human, and therefore subject to stresses of body, mind, emotions, and spirit.

I forgive that I sometimes react to stresses in ways that are not useful. Through my forgiveness, I build the strength to find more useful ways to react.

I forgive myself. I love myself. I forgive myself.

Dates:

Monday

Find ten minutes when you will be uninterrupted. Follow the directions on the opposite page for the Circle of Breath exercise.

Tuesday

Write this on your mirror: I feel perfect serenity flowing through me.

Wednesday

Take ten minutes to relax. Breathe slowly and deeply and clear your mind of all distracting thoughts. When you feel relaxed, rotate your shoulders in large, smooth circles.

Thursday

Write this on your mirror: I am able to see things from a calm perspective.

Friday

When something can always irritate us, we say it "pushes our buttons." Close your eyes and visualize a cover fitting over such a button inside of you so that it can no longer be pushed.

Saturday

Write this on your mirror: I am in control of my own thoughts and actions.

Sunday

Do something today that is healthy for you, even if it is a part of your daily routine. Think about how you choose to bring health to your life.

Circle of Breath Exercise

Do this exercise slowly and evenly, pausing between each inhalation and exhalation.

1. Stand with your feet about hip width apart.

2. Hold your hands over your heart.

3. Inhale as you raise your arms, stretching your hands over your head about shoulder width apart, palms facing up. Pause for a few seconds.

4. Hold this position as you slowly exhale. Pause for a few seconds.

5. Inhale again as you lower your arms. Place your hands over your solar plexus (where your ribs separate below your sternum). Pause for a few seconds.

6. Exhale as you draw your hands back up to place them over your heart. Pause for a few seconds.

Repeat these movements five to ten times, until you feel filled with energy.

Dates:

Monday

On the opposite page, write one sentence about how you or a part of you is like the sun.

Tuesday

On the opposite page, write one sentence about how you or a part of you is like the earth.

Wednesday

On the opposite page, write one sentence about how you or a part of you is like the seas.

Thursday

On the opposite page, write one sentence about how you or a part of you is like the moon.

Friday

On the opposite page, write one sentence about how you or a part of you is like the stars.

Saturday

On the opposite page, write one sentence about how you or a part of you is like the air.

Sunday

Read what you have written on the opposite page. Take ten minutes to think about how the elements that are in you are the same elements in everything in the universe.

Dates:

Monday

Give yourself a foot bath with hot water and ginger. Follow this by massaging your feet. Mentally thank them for all their hard work.

Tuesday

Write this on your mirror: I am free to think whatever I wish.

Wednesday

On the opposite page, draw what you'd look like if you were a plant.

Thursday

Write this on your mirror: I have a wise teacher inside myself.

Friday

Take fifteen minutes to sit quietly and watch out your window. Try to free your thoughts from everything but simply observing what you see.

Saturday

Write this on your mirror: I release myself from misperceptions from my childhood.

Sunday

Find a place where you can watch the sunset. Clear your mind of the day's events and simply watch the colors of the sky change.

Dates:

Monday

Write this on your mirror: I attract people who care about me.

Tuesday

What does it mean to give someone a break? Take five minutes to think about how you can give someone a break.

Wednesday

Write this on your mirror: I am a positive influence in other people's lives.

Thursday

Write a note to someone you work with or with whom you share work. Tell them one thing you appreciate about her or his work style.

Friday

Write this on your mirror: My opinion of myself is the only one that really matters.

Saturday

Read the message from the Wise Ones on the opposite page. How can you bring freedom to your thoughts?

Sunday

Write this on your mirror: I deserve respect.

Message from The Wise Ones

Few on earth believe that they are capable of changing their lives, for they see life as the "outside world" and they do not see the correlation between their thoughts, their world outside, and their lives.

Therefore, we ask that people consider the notion of creating a new world from the inside out. Consider your own perceptions and your ability to choose, control, and be in command of yourself with the power of your spirit and the vehicle of your mind.

Dates:

Monday

Sing along with the radio or a recording. Open your throat and let deep joy come from your voice.

Tuesday

Write this on your mirror: I know how to have fun!

Wednesday

Wish upon a star tonight.

Thursday

Write this on your mirror: I am admirable.

Friday

Whom do you admire? Take a few minutes to think about which qualities of yours are like the qualities of the one you admire.

Saturday

Write this on your mirror: I dissolve any feelings of envy I have for others.

Sunday

On the opposite page, list five ways you personally honor God, however you define God.

Dates:

Monday

Write this on your mirror: I can accomplish great things.

Tuesday

Plant something from a seed or begin a new plant from a leaf clipping. Think about the miracle of regeneration and growth.

Wednesday

Write this on your mirror: I am patient with my own growth process.

Thursday

Today, eat foods that will give you more energy and fewer toxins.

Friday

Write this on your mirror: I am able to listen to my own emotions without fear.

Saturday

On the opposite page, write your thoughts about the last time you felt deeply moved.

Sunday

Write this on your mirror: I base my actions on clear priorities I have for my life.

Dates:

Monday

When you are outside today, take deep breaths of air through your nose and mouth. What do you smell and taste?

Tuesday

Write this on your mirror: It is natural for me to feel inner harmony.

Wednesday

Sit quietly for ten minutes. Focus your attention on the things you can hear. Listen for loud and soft sounds, nature and human sounds. Put all your attention in your sense of hearing.

Thursday

Write this on your mirror: I am able to release all resentment toward others.

Friday

On the opposite page, draw a picture of what it would look like if all pain could be released from your body.

Saturday

Write this on your mirror: I am always protected by Divine Energy and Love.

Sunday

Light a candle and dedicate its flame to peace on earth. Place the candle near a window so that its light shines forth from your home.

Dates:

Monday

Write this on your mirror: My imagination has no boundaries.

Tuesday

Call a friend or a loved one you trust. Share your thoughts about your deepest desire for your immediate future.

Wednesday

Write this on your mirror: I have deep sources of creativity in my soul.

Thursday

On the opposite page, draw what you think your imagination looks like.

Friday

Write this on your mirror: I fill my mind with interesting thoughts.

Saturday

Take ten minutes to think about what these sentences means to you: "My mind is part of God's mind. Therefore, whatever I can imagine, God can create."

Sunday

Write this on your mirror: I grow more personally powerful every day.

Dates:

Monday

On the opposite page, write one reason your eyes are beautiful.

Tuesday

On the opposite page, write one way your body works well.

Wednesday

On the opposite page, write the most recent compliment someone gave you.

Thursday

On the opposite page, write one statement about your best physical feature.

Friday

On the opposite page, write one thing your hands do well.

Saturday

On the opposite page, write the best thing about your smile.

Sunday

Read the statements you've written on the opposite page about your physical self. Take ten minutes to reflect on what it means to be made "in God's image."

Dates:

Monday

Write this on your mirror: It's a pleasure being me.

Tuesday

Drink twice as much water as you normally do. Focus on this as a way to flush toxins from your system.

Wednesday

Write this on your mirror: My actions show that I have a high regard for myself.

Thursday

Read the Morning Meditation out loud as you sit in a relaxed, peaceful place.

Friday

Write this on your mirror: Joy and happiness are rightfully mine.

Saturday

Do a favor for someone who is pressed for time.

Sunday

Write this on your mirror: I respect my spiritual nature.

Morning Meditation

White Light Prayer

The Light is surrounding me, the Light is protecting me, the Light is consuming me.

Divine Love is flowing in and through me, solving and dissolving all situations for the good of all.

A Higher Power is in charge of my life, and only good can come to me and through me.

My mind is open, my heart is receptive, and miracles are happening to me right now.

Thank you.

Affirmation for Today

Today is filled with possibilities.

I choose options which lead toward love, joy, forgiveness, health, prosperity, and peace.

I have many resources, both within and outside myself to draw on.

I am filled with power to reach my goals.

Dates:

Monday

Give someone a hug today. As you embrace, think about the positive, happy energy that is flowing between and around you.

Tuesday

Write this on your mirror: I like the way I look.

Wednesday

On the opposite page, write your thoughts about what wonderful things a robot would miss by not being human.

Thursday

Write this on your mirror: I enjoy being human.

Friday

Wiggle your fingers and toes. Bend your elbows and knees. Rotate your hips, shoulders, and neck. Notice how well your body joints are engineered.

Saturday

Write this on your mirror: I release shame from any past mistakes I may have made.

Sunday

Stand in front of the mirror and repeat the following phrase, filling in the blank: "I'm so glad that I _______ ." Repeat it with a different fill-in at least seven times.

Dates:

Monday

Write this on your mirror: I am wonderful!

Tuesday

Talk to your plants when you water them this week.

Wednesday

Write this on your mirror: I easily draw upon inner resources to make my life better.

Thursday

To experience the guided visualization on the opposite page, either memorize the steps, read them into a tape recorder and play them back to yourself, or have someone read them to you.

Friday

Write this on your mirror: I broadcast loving acceptance of myself and others.

Saturday

Find a quiet place where you will be uninterrupted. Think about a specific person or group of people who are suffering. Create a prayer for their freedom.

Sunday

Write this on your mirror: I follow a spiritual path.

Guided Visualization

Relax, relax. Close your eyes and feel yourself sink into the center of your being. (Pause)

Find yourself along the shore of an ocean or a large lake. What can you see? Are there trees and plants? What colors do you see in the water? (Pause)

Sit along the shore. Notice the texture of the shore. What does it feel like? (Pause)

Do you hear bird cries? The sound of waves lapping to the shore? What do you hear? (Pause)

Can you smell the odors of water and vegetation? What do you smell right now? (Pause)

Open your mouth to the wind. What flavors are borne on the breezes? (Pause)

Look out to the water. Slowly coming toward you, rising from the water, is a woman. She is dressed in beautiful robes. Look at her coming slowly toward you. What colors is she wearing? What does she look like? (Pause)

As she comes nearer, she holds out her right hand. She gives you a flower. What kind of flower is it? (Pause)

She holds out her left hand and offers you a gift. Take the gift. What is her gift to you? (Pause)

She smiles and returns slowly to the sea. Watch her leave, and then slowly come back to this room. (Pause)

What do the symbols of the kind of flower and gift she gave mean to you? Think about these gifts, and think how you'll use them today.

Dates:

Monday

On the opposite page, list three ways to make your home environment reflect the beauty of nature.

Tuesday

Write this on your mirror: I have an interesting life.

Wednesday

With a friend or loved one, play the following game. Say to the other, "You have a great life because _____ ." Alternate filing in the blank for as long as you can.

Thursday

Write this on your mirror: I am fun to be around.

Friday

Sit quietly for ten minutes. Imagine that you are a seed. See yourself sprouting and growing strong and beautiful. Later, think about what you grew into and what it symbolized to you.

Saturday

Write this on your mirror: I choose my actions based on future dreams rather than past pain.

Sunday

Listen to music with strong rhythms. As you dance to it, try to feel the rhythms deep inside your body.

Dates:

Monday

Write this on your mirror: I am fascinating.

Tuesday

Tell someone your fantasy for a perfect vacation.

Wednesday

Write this on your mirror: My heart is open to love.

Thursday

Think about a discouraging incident from your past. How did it contribute to who you are now? Say out loud, "I like myself. I am grateful to have learned from the past to be who I am now."

Friday

Write this on your mirror: I see new depths in my character.

Saturday

Choose any writing assignment from the first pages in this workbook. Do it again on the opposite page. Compare the two, and think about the ways you've grown this year.

Sunday

Write this on your mirror: I choose to cast out useless fears from my life.

Dates:

Monday

What do you do because you think you ***should***? Think about ***who*** says you should. Can you think of a good reason you choose to do it? If not, decide how to stop doing it.

Tuesday

Write this on your mirror: I let go of hostility.

Wednesday

Think about someone you feel negatively about. Visualize putting those feelings into a trash can. In the space where those feelings used to be, visualize a beautiful blue light.

Thursday

Write this on your mirror: I choose to behave ethically.

Friday

At the end of the day, think about every person you interacted with today. How did you affect each other's moods and actions?

Saturday

Write this on your mirror: The power of Goodness works through me.

Sunday

Read the quote by Blaise Pascal on the opposite page. What does it mean to you today?

It is the heart which
experiences God,
and not the reason.

This, then, is faith:
God felt by the heart,
not by the reason.

Blaise Pascal

Dates:

Monday

Write this on your mirror: My will power comes from a holy source deep within myself.

Tuesday

Give thanks for your food. Today, add a separate blessing for each kind of food you eat.

Wednesday

Write this on your mirror: I am creative.

Thursday

On the opposite page, list three acts of kindness you have performed recently.

Friday

Write this on your mirror: I am proud of myself.

Saturday

Wear something you consider special. Do it as an act of self esteem.

Sunday

Write this on your mirror: I am wise.

Dates:

Monday

Find a natural object, such as a stone or a feather. Hold it in both hands and say, "Each time I see this, I'll remember to listen to my heart's wisdom." Put it where you'll see it often.

Tuesday

Write this on your mirror: My dreams for the future can be achieved.

Wednesday

Wear a different combination of clothes and accessories than you have ever worn before.

Thursday

Write this on your mirror: I give myself permission to try.

Friday

On the opposite page, draw an abstract "collage of life." Use colors and shapes to symbolize what you feel are important aspects of life.

Saturday

Write this on your mirror: I easily transform limiting thoughts to self-loving thoughts.

Sunday

Sit quietly for ten minutes. Close your eyes and breathe deeply and slowly. Repeat to yourself as you breathe, "I inhale love, I exhale fear."

Dates:

Monday

Write this on your mirror: I can have what I really want.

Tuesday

On the opposite page, list three things you no longer need.

Wednesday

Write this on your mirror: I project loving thoughts outward toward everyone and inward to myself.

Thursday

The Gaia Hypothesis says the earth itself is a living entity. Take fifteen minutes to think about how the earth breathes, nourishes and cleanses itself, circulates energy, and evolves.

Friday

Write this on your mirror: I have the power to feel peaceful.

Saturday

What odors do you like? Baking bread or cookies? A particular kind of soap or lotion? Growing plants? Make plans to smell that odor today as a gift to yourself.

Sunday

Write this on your mirror: The world needs people like me.

Dates:

Monday

What's a good flavor for today's weather? Hot cocoa on a cold day? A frozen pop on a hot day? Soup on a rainy day? Decide what would be today's perfect flavor and serve it to yourself.

Tuesday

Write this on your mirror: Inner beauty shapes all my smiles.

Wednesday

Make an appointment to have a professional massage or facial. As you feel another's hands relax you, focus on the relaxing energy she or he transfers to you.

Thursday

Write this on your mirror: I listen to my inner judgment and choose my actions accordingly.

Friday

Gaze at the night sky tonight and look for patterns and pictures in the stars or the clouds.

Saturday

Write this on your mirror: I have artistic abilities which are reflected in my daily work.

Sunday

Follow the directions for the Grounding Exercise on the opposite page.

Morning Grounding Exercise

Breathe slowly and deeply three times, feeling how well your lungs, heart, and muscles work together.

Still breathing slowly and deeply, put your attention in your feet, then legs, then hips, and so on up your body until your attention is in your brain.

As you focus attention on various body parts, concentrate on how they serve you. If your thoughts stray to something you dislike or is dysfunctional about a particular body part, gently bring your thoughts and attitude back to tones of love and gratitude for what it can do for you.

When you have finished, imagine Divine Energy flooding through the top of your head and flowing down through your entire body until you are completely filled.

Smile, give thanks, and begin your day.

Dates:

Monday

Write this on your mirror: I am honorable.

Tuesday

Find a recording you haven't listened to in years. Dance to it the way you used to.

Wednesday

Write this on your mirror: The past is over. I release anger for past events.

Thursday

Write a letter to someone you have been angry with. Let your feelings flow on the paper. Do not mail the letter. Burn it and imagine your feelings are released by the flames.

Friday

Write this on your mirror: My mind is sharp.

Saturday

On the opposite page, list five good ideas you've had recently.

Sunday

Write this on your mirror: Peace and happiness surround me.

Dates:

Monday

Give the gift of your time or money to a cause that supports social concerns.

Tuesday

Write this on your mirror: I receive many gifts from the universe.

Wednesday

On the opposite page, write your thoughts about how you've used your talents.

Thursday

Write this on your mirror: I make effective choices for improving my life.

Friday

Turn to the second week's exercise in this book and read your goals for your inner self. Are they the same? How have you approached those goals over the last months? Take a few minutes to think about your own inner growth.

Saturday

Write this on your mirror: I feel vitality in every cell of my body.

Sunday

Eat one meal today in complete silence. Use the quiet time to reflect on the pleasure and energy each food item gives you.

Dates:

Monday

Write this on your mirror: My life offers many opportunities for pleasure.

Tuesday

On the opposite page, write your thoughts about how your concept of forgiveness changed over this year.

Wednesday

Write this on your mirror: I am fortunate.

Thursday

Tell someone one reason you feel blessed.

Friday

Write this on your mirror: I am tranquil.

Saturday

Find a picture of earth taken from space. Take a few minutes to think about how many miracles had to happen for our jewel of a planet to emerge from darkness.

Sunday

Write this on your mirror: I reflect Divine magnificence.

Dates:

Monday

On the opposite page, write one positive change you made this year.

Tuesday

On the opposite page, write one new thing you tried this year.

Wednesday

On the opposite page, write one gift you gave to another recently.

Thursday

On the opposite page, write one new insight you've had about your life.

Friday

On the opposite page, write one project you accomplished this year.

Saturday

On the opposite page, write the best fun time you had this year.

Sunday

Read the statements you've written on the opposite page. Now take ten minutes to think about your special journey this year, and congratulate yourself.

Other Yes Publications

Mirrors: Affirmations & Actions for Daily Reflection by Cheryl Wall. 11.95

Mirrors for Men by Justin O'Brien & Charles Bates. 11.96.

Pigs Eat Wolves: Going into Partnership with Your Dark Side by Charles Bates. 9.95.

The Wellness Tree: Energizing Yourself in Body, Mind, and Spirit by Justin O'Brien. 15.95.

Ransoming the Mind: An Integration of Yoga and Modern Therapy by Charles Bates. 11.95

The Spiral Path: Essays and Interviews on Women's Spirituality by Theresa King O'Brien. 15.95

Cassette Tape Courses:

A Life in Harmony: Introduction to Holistic Spirituality. Justin O'Brien. 4 tapes, 40.00

The Art of Stillness: Meditation for Christians. Justin O'Brien. 4 tapes, 40.00

Transforming the Self: Creative Techniques for Personal Development. O'Brien. 4 tapes, 40.00.

Sleepless Sleep: The Art of Conscious Rest. Justin O'Brien. 4 tapes, 40.00.

The Wonder of Living. Justin O'Brien. 4 tapes 40.00.

Putting Your Body in Your Life: A Course in Body Awareness. Charles Bates. 4 tapes, 40.00.

Meditation: The Next Step for Humankind: Beginning Course. Charles Bates. 12 tapes, 98.00.

Meditation: The Next Step for Humankind: Intermediate Course. Charles Bates. 8 tapes, 80.00.

Single Cassette Instructional Tapes:

001 Progressive Relaxation. O'Brien. 10.00

002 Breathing I. O'Brien. 10.00

003 Meditation. O'Brien. 10.00

004 Energizing for Creativity and the 61 Points. O'Brien. 10.00.

005 Stretching for Life. O'Brien. 10.00.

006 Strive Without Stress I. O'Brien. 10.00.

007 Strive Without Stress II. O'Brien. 10.00.

008 Get to Sleep! O'Brien. 6.00.

009 Intermediate Breathing and Relaxation. O'Brien. 10.00

100 Beginning Hatha Yoga Postures. Bates. 10.00.

101 Breathing I. Bates. 10.00.

102 Breathing II. Bates. 10.00.

103 Relaxation I and II. Bates. 10.00.

104 Relaxation and Music. Bates. 10.00.

105 61 Points and Yoga Practice. Bates. 10.00.

106 Meditation and Yoga Practice. Bates. 10.00.

107 Intermediate Hatha Yoga Postures. Bates. 10.00.

108 Joints and Glands Exercises. Bates. 10.00.

To order any of the above publications, send listed price plus 2.00 postage to YES International Publishers, P.O. Box 75032, Saint Paul, MN 55175-0032. Call 612-293-8094 for free catalog.